# WOMEN LIVES MATTER

TODAY AND TOMORROW

## LOTTIE L. ADAMS

Jacksonville, AR

ISBN 9781089396314 Print Edition

# CONTENTS

Illustrated by Alana Nicole Harris

# ACKNOWLEDGEMENTS

Thank you to the Traditionalist and Baby Boomer Women who shared their life experiences through written and personal interviews. Without your input, this book would not have been possible. I want to express my appreciation for all contributions that supported this book. It has been a pleasure to work with such a great support group.

A special thank-you is extended to my children: Sonya, Carla, Latricia, and Benjamin for their encouragement and patience.

# FOREWORD

While writing this book, the greatest inspiration was encouragement from the visionary women of the Traditionalist and Baby Boomer Generations. The character of these women was evident from their immediate response to the survey. All life experiences shared by these visionary women were appreciated and were recorded in this book.

## PREFACE

Women Lives Matter is written to share life experiences from Traditionalist and Baby Boomer Women. These two generations shared their life experiences about culture, character, prized possessions, and biggest inspiration. Primarily, this book is designed for women between 18 and 35 years. They can utilize these experiences to value their role in the family and in society. Finally, these younger women may be inspired to pass this wealth of knowledge on to future generations.

PROLOGUE

# PROLOGUE

Information about life situations can provide knowledge from past experiences and help shape the future of younger women. Younger women should be inspired to utilize the information to reach greater heights in their life. This book shares the legacy of two intergenerational groups of women. Women from the Traditionalists and Baby Boomers Generation were selected, surveyed, and their valuable information will be shared with women between 18 and 35 years. The Traditionalist and the Baby Boomer Women have created a legacy for the generation of women between 18 and 35 years. These visionary women provide strong family structures with great integrity, and they are committed to influencing all generations.

*"Life is our dictionary."*

-Ralph Waldo Emerson

# INTRODUCTION

Michelle Tea (2015) has suggested, "Perhaps some of us have glided into adulthood with all the grace of a swan, skimming lightly into an adult living situation, adult relationship, adult jobs and income." Although Tea introduced individuals to the comical side of growing up, adulthood can be challenging. Furthermore, Tea (2015) contended that "most important, individuals may have glided into an adult sense of confidence, of a solid place in the world of stability." There are other ways of learning about adulthood and life-lesson challenges.

One question for women between 18 and 35 years should be how to make responsible decisions. Next, how Great-grandmother, Grandmother, and Mother navigated through their life experiences. Women could benefit from lessons they learn from other generations and share this wealth of knowledge. Women of all culture groups share various life experiences and challenging situations. Some life experiences that women share include the following situations: family, education, religion and spiritual concerns, determination, and perseverance. Life experiences that bind women together are challenges, compassion, fairness, love and kindness, relationships, and values.

Barr (2017) asked, what's the difference between a life vision and long-term goals? Goals are individual experiences and accomplishments strived for. A vision is the bigger picture. He suggested that life's vision defines who an individual wants to be, what one wants to be known for and the set of experiences and accomplishments one aims for. According to Barr (2017, p. 2) one's vision helps define the goals by giving an individual a framework to evaluate those goals. He suggested one's vision should aim to answer these questions:

1. What does an individual believe they're capable of in life?

2. What are the greatest things one could accomplish, given the right circumstances, resources, and motivation?

3. What could one contribute to the world that would make them feel proud and content? (p.2)

Traditionalist and Baby Boomer Generations span from 1925 to 1964. These groups are family and work oriented. They provide experience, knowledge, and wisdom to influence younger generations. These women are identified by their character attributes, morals and ethics. Visionary women from these two generations are capable and eager to support younger women by sharing the best advice they ever received, describing their character attributes, identifying their most prized possessions, and explaining their biggest inspiration.

# TRADITIONALIST

*"The more you know of your history, the more liberated you are."*

\- Maya Angelou

# WHO ARE THE TRADITIONALISTS?

"Traditionalist men and women were born between 1922 and 1945. Also, the Traditionalist generation were known as veterans, the Silent Generation and the Greatest Generation. These older Americans hold three-quarters of the nation's wealth. This group survived the Great Depression of the 1930s. They believed in patriotism, teamwork, doing more with less and a task orientation defines this generation. They have rules of conduct, respect for authority, and following directions. They are true innovators. They are responsible for developing today's space program, creating vaccines for many diseases including polio, tuberculosis, tetanus, and whooping cough and laying the foundation for today's technological environment." (ValueOptions, 2017)

**Silent Generation 1925–1945**

Silent Gens are the youngest of the Traditionalists. They are the original sandwich generation, as they found themselves smushed between the war-hero Greatest Gen and the many Baby Boomers. While most were too young to fight in World War II, they were in the midst of their early formative years during the Great Depression and the Dust Bowl, and they were eventually drafted for the Korean War. While adults of the time recited that children were to be seen and not heard, this segment of Traditionalists learned to keep to themselves.

In 1951, TIME Magazine described the Silent Generation as unimaginative, withdrawn, unadventurous, and cautious, but upon transitioning into adulthood, this gen developed ambitions to rise above their losses from the Great Depression, Dust Bowl, and World War II, and they went on to raise about half of Gen X, our beloved modern sandwich generation.

They moved families from farms and cities to a new kind of community—suburbia. This generation was the first to pursue equality through the Civil Rights Movement. The Traditionalist values and work style are evident by the chart below:

# Silent Generation/Traditionalists (born before 1946)

| Who? | Population | Characteristics | At Work | Historic Events |
|---|---|---|---|---|
| • Grew up during the Great Depression and WWII | • 55 million | • Behaviors are based on experiences from the Depression | • Loyal to employers and expect the same in return | • Great Depression |
| • Either fought in WWII or were children | • Majority are retirees | • Want to feel needed | | • WWII |
| • Behaviors are based on experiences during the Depression and WWII | • Largest voting population | • Strive for financial security | • Possess superb interpersonal skills | • The Cold War |
| • Wealthiest generation | | • "Waste not want not" attitude | •Enjoy flexible arrangements so they can work on their own schedule | • McCarthyism |
| • Men typically worked while women stayed home to raise children | | • Conformity | | • Started the Civil Rights Movement |
| • Has largest lobbyist group, AARP | | • Conservatism | • Believe promotions, raises, and recognition should come from job tenure | • Children were "seen, but not heard" |
| | | • Traditional family values | | |
| | | • Strive for comfort | | |
| | | • Demand quality | | |
| | | • Simplicity | | |
| | | • Understands the nobility of sacrifice for the common good | • Measure work ethic on timeliness, productivity, and not drawing attention | |
| | | • Patriotic | | |
| | | • Patience | | |
| | | • Team players | | |

Source: http://www.marstoncomm.com/matures.html; http://merrillassociates.com/

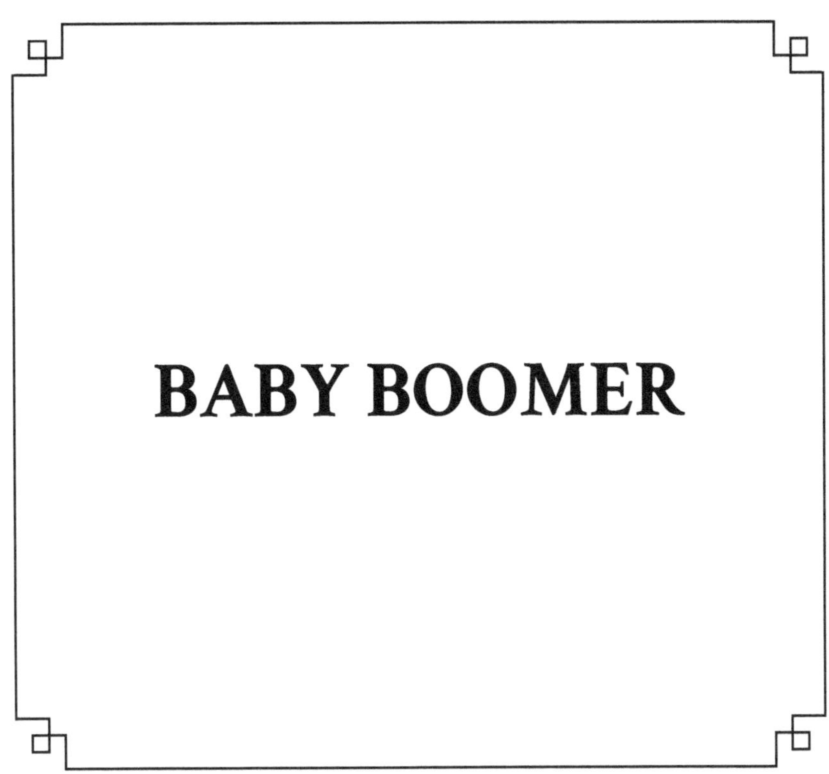

BABY BOOMER

*"You get whatever accomplishment you are willing to declare."*
-Georgia O'Keeffe

# WHO ARE THE BABY BOOMERS?

During the Boomer birth years of 1946–1964, a baby was born every eight seconds. The label "baby boom" is more than apt for this large generation of 80 million. By 1964, they comprised 40% of the U.S. population (ValueOptions, 2017). Their huge population size and the booming post-war economy proved to be enormously influential conditions as Boomers came of age.

The Baby Boomer Generation is often portrayed as a generation of optimism, exploration and achievement. Compared with previous generations, more young adults pursued higher education or relocated away from family to pursue career and educational interests (ValueOptions, 2017). The Baby Boomer Generation witnessed and participated in some of the greatest social changes in the country's history during the 1960s and 1970s with the Civil Rights Movement and the Women's Movement. This generation experienced dramatic shifts in educational, economic and social opportunities (ValueOptions, 2017).

# PLACE OF BIRTH

"You cannot swim for new horizons
until you have courage to lose sight
of the shore."

–William Faulkner

## The Movement Generation

Boomers were (and are) galvanized by a spirit of change. That belief in their ability to effect positive change, paired with momentous U.S. victories like man landing on the moon, equipped this generation with an idealistic and optimistic spirit.

Although men and women make up the Traditionalist and Baby Boomer Generations, this survey was distributed to women. The results of the findings were focused on visionary women from the Traditionalist and Baby Boomer Generations.

Five survey questions were designed and distributed to participants from the Traditionalist and Baby Boomer Generations. The five effective questions that should increase the knowledge of 18- to 35-year-old women about life experiences were as follows:

1. Name the state where they were born.

2. Share the best advice they ever received.

3. Describe their character in one word.

4. Share some insight about what they considered their most prized  possession.

5. List and explain their biggest inspiration.

Through their responses, the intent was for these women to share some life experiences. These intergenerational women shared and presented life-changing experiences for women 18-35 years, and future generations.

**Definitions:**

The terms used in this survey were birthplace, origin, advice, character, possession, and inspiration (Random House Unabridged Dictionary, 2001).

- Birthplace - place of birth or origin (p. 213)
- Origin - Something from which anything rises or is derived. Source. The first of its existence; beginning (p. 1366)
- Advice - An opinion or recommendation offered as a guide to action, conduct (p. 29)
- Character - The aggregate of features and traits that form the individual nature of some person or thing (p. 346)
- Possession - To maintain control over, have as property, own, to dominate, to occupy or hold (p. 1533)
- Inspiration - To inspire. To influence or impel (p. 987)

## BIRTH STATES OF PARTICIPANTS:

- Arkansas
- California
- Illinois
- Louisiana
- New Jersey
- North Carolina
- Ohio
- Pennsylvania
- Tennessee
- Texas
- Washington DC
- Washington State

***Some Traditionalists and Baby Boomers were born in the same state. The states are listed only once and in alphabetical order.**

Although the Traditionalist and Baby Boomer Women were represented by twelve birthplace states, this book does not focus on birthplace or on order of birth. Women were asked this question to determine if there were similarities and differences in the reported responses. One significant finding indicated that regardless of their birthplace, *Womens Lives Matter: Today and Tomorrow.*

# BEST ADVICE
# RECEIVED

*"To advise is not to compel."*

–Anton Chekhov

# BEST ADVICE EVER RECEIVED

- Don't worry about things you can't change, for worrying has never changed anything.
- Treat everyone like you want to be treated.
- If you don't stand for something you will fall for anything.
- Treat people the way you want to be treated.
- How to become a Christian.
- My grandfather was an advocate for education and he advised to get an education in which no one could take from me. He stated, with an education, you could go places in life.
- My mother taught us that we are no better than anyone else and no one else is better than us. My siblings and I still abide by this rule.
- From my granddad, speak up for yourself; from my mom, there's nowhere to hide.
- Help those that cannot help themselves.
- Two women encouraged me to pursue a teaching career in education. Retirement is great and it is one of the rewards.
- You are going to be anything you want to be. Throughout my life, as I accomplished more and more of my dreams and when I doubted myself, I remembered how many times this had been true.
- Treat others the way you would like to be treated. Be yourself and be sincere. Stand for what you believe in.
- Learn all you can. Stay in school.
- Be proactive: Whatever the situation, it applies.
- Be grateful. Concentrate on what you have rather than what you don't have.

- Do your very best at whatever job you have; you know you will not please everyone.
- The road to self-fulfillment is through what you can contribute to others. Do unto others as you would have them do unto you. The importance of listening to and respecting others and then meeting them where they are without judging.
- The concept of deep listening as taught in *7 Habits of Highly Effective People* (Covey, 1989). It was transforming to understand the importance of blocking my own opinions and ideas to focus totally on what someone else was saying.
- Forgive and God will forgive you.
- It is more blessed to give than to receive.
- Don't try to be anyone else but you. Don't compare myself to anyone else: Be me.
- Count your blessings. Live with an attitude of gratitude for today and faith in tomorrow.
- You are the best; be it.
- Always do your best; that is good enough. If you want to get out of the cotton patch, you must get something in your head. Always speak the truth; the day you see the truth and refuse to speak is the day you began to die. Never give up your tomorrows worrying about yesterday.
- Love your siblings because they will always be there for you. Make a dollar, save a dime. Later, I learned to love myself first and other things will come together (if possible).
- You can be anything you want to be, if you are willing to work for it.
- Be yourself; no one can beat you being you. I have lived by this adage.

- To always pursue your education as its value is unsurpassed and can never be taken from you. Lifelong learning is a value that will be passed on to your loved ones and generations to come.

- If a grievance is more than a year old, drop it. Don't grab-bag and bring up stuff from the past. Deal with problems as they arise, but don't keep going to the past hunting hurts.

- My best advice came from my mother: Please get your education. At the time, I didn't understand, but I now understand. Mother was so right, in the world we live in today, as women, single or married, it is very difficult to make ends meet. Advice to younger women: Get your education before marriage and family.

The Serenity Prayer by Reinhold Niebuhr (1892-1971) Complete, Unabridged, Original Version.

> *God, give us grace to accept with serenity*
> *the things that cannot be changed,*
> *Courage to change the things*
> *which should be changed,*
> *and the Wisdom to distinguish*
> *the one from the other.*

- My grandmother said treat people the way you want to be treated. That advice was foremost in my mind throughout my life and career and served me well. Regardless of a person's work/career status, they are all valuable and have something to offer. From the janitor who cleaned the building, to the clerk in the office or the waitress who serves your food or the person who washes the dishes at the restaurant. Also, the teacher who took you places in books you could only dream about. What about the neighbor who was too ashamed for you to come into their home. God loved each and every one equally. Grandmother always said one would never know who would someday have to come to their rescue. It costs nothing to be nice or to offer words of encouragement. Smiles and respect are free. Being kind and generous will leave a lasting impact on others. It will improve your health, and unlock doors you thought would never open.

- Keep God first in my life, and treat people the way you would want to be treated.
- How beautiful it is to stay silent, when someone else expects you to be enraged.
- Make God your first priority in all that you do. Do not bring dishonor to your family. Always wear clean underwear.
- Use your talent for the benefit of others. I was encouraged to always trust God.
- A conscience is a terrible thing to waste. Your conscience is your alarm system; listen to it carefully.
- To thine own self, be true.

Advice is defined as an opinion about what could or should be done about a situation or problem; counsel (American Heritage Dictionary, 2016).

Twenty-two of the nation's most interesting and accomplished shared words of wisdom that changed their lives. These individuals included bestselling authors, cutting-edge entrepreneurs, humanitarians, educators, entertainers, and doctors. They answered the question, what is the best advice they ever received? (Gelman, 2015, p. 41). They shared information on confrontation, winning, caring, uncertainty, assumptions, listening, burnout, time management, and fourteen other topics. Although the question about the best advice ever received was asked and published in the *Reader's Digest*, it remains a relevant question today. This book explores one of the same questions: what is the best advice that women from the Traditionalist and Baby Boomer Generations ever received? These intergenerational women shared this information to encourage and perhaps influence women between 18 and 35 years of age.

# CHARACTER DESCRIPTION

*"Well done is better than well said."*

–Benjamin Franklin

## CHARACTER DESCRIPTION (IN ONE WORD)

The list is formatted to emphasize and describe the following attributes of Traditionalists and Baby Boomers:

| | | |
|---|---|---|
| Altruistic | Energetic | Nurturing |
| Balanced | Enthusiastic | Outspoken |
| Caring | Faithful | Peacemaker |
| Compassionate | Friendly | Realist |
| Creative | Generous | Reserved |
| Dependable | Godly | Sincere |
| Determined | Honest | Supportive |
| Diplomatic | Integrity | Thankful |
| Dramatic | Loyal | Truthful |

**List 1.2 Character Description in One Word**

***Note. Some participants described the same character descriptions:**

The Traditionalists, sometimes called the Silent Generation, and Baby Boomers used a broad range of terms to describe their character. Some women noted the same attributes.

Although some character descriptions were noted and recorded more than once, there were no data shown to differentiate between the two groups to denote the similarities and differences between the Traditionalist and Baby Boomer.

Character is defined as the combination of mental characteristics and behavior that distinguishes a person or group (American Heritage Dictionary, 2016). Some of these women's attributes were: compassionate, determined, faithful, loyal, persistent, and a realist. American Heritage Dictionary defines compassionate as sympathetic; faithful is adhering firmly and devotedly, as to a person, cause, or idea. Loyal is steadfast in allegiance. Faithful to a person, ideal, custom, cause, or duty. Persistent is defined as refusing to give up or let go. Persevering, insistently repetitive or continuous, enduring. Realist is defined as one who is inclined to literal truth and pragmatism (See table 1.1).

According to ValueOptions (2019) the characteristics of Traditionalists and Baby Boomers are described by their values and attributes in the workplace.

## CHARACTERISTICS OF TRADITIONAL AND BABY BOOMER GENERATION WORKERS: (SEE TABLE 1.2)

|  | Traditionalists | Baby Boomers |
| --- | --- | --- |
| Birth Years | 1900-1945 | 1946-1964 |
| Current Age range in 2019 | 74-119 | 55-73 |
| Values | - Conformity, Authority, and Rules<br>- Believe in Logic<br>- Very defined sense of right and wrong<br>- Loyalty and respect for authority | - Individual choice<br>- Community involvement<br>- Prosperity<br>- Ownership<br>- Self-actualizing<br>- Health and wellness |
| Attributes | - Disciplined<br>- View an understanding of history as a way to plan for the future<br>- Dislike conflict<br>- Detail Oriented | - Adaptive<br>- Goal-Oriented<br>- Focus on individual choices and freedom<br>- Positive attitude |

Source: http://www.valueoptions.com/spotlight_YIW/traditional.htm Retrieved 7/23/19

# MOST PRIZED POSSESSION

*"The secret of getting ahead is getting started."*

–Mark Twain

# MOST PRIZED POSSESSIONS

- My family and extended family. Good health and my children
- A music/jewelry box I got at age ten from my brother who is deceased
- My wedding rings
- Life and health
- My grandmother's china
- Family pictures
- My wedding rings
- A gold watch from my deceased husband
- My library
- A good foundation
- Having faith in God
- My family (husband, children, and grandchildren)
- My Meissen Porcelain figurines that my German relatives sent my grandparents that belonged to my dad. Christmas ornaments made by my children, and my mother's paintings
- Photographs of family, friends and experiences
- A brass bell with a worn wooden handle used by my paternal great-grandmother to call for help as she lay dying of tuberculosis: This was in their modest sod house on the Minnesota Prairie; the same prairie where I grew up.
- Salvation
- Older photos of my children growing up
- A family photo with all twelve siblings in it. Five siblings are deceased (tangible). My Faith (intangible).
- The love of my children
- Jewelry from my mother and grandmother; the pieces are not valuable, but I think of them when I wear it.

- My five great-grandchildren
- Life experiences
- A cedar Hope Chest with leather seating. I received it from my mother at the age of 16 years. I still have it at the foot of my bed. It contains remnants of my dreams and successes.
- I'm not sure of a prized possession.
- Great friends
- My prize possessions are the love of God and friends.
- My prize possessions are my children.
- A book of daily meditations given to me when my husband died. The book is titled, *Listening to Your Life* by Frederick Buechner.

Prize possessions is to value highly; esteem or treasure. Power or control over something. Something worth striving for (American Heritage Dictionary, 2016). After reviewing the responses from Traditionalist and Baby Boomer Women regarding what they consider their prized possession, it is evident that family and other relationships are of great value and are treasured. When material items such as photos, jewelry, books, paintings, and other heirlooms are mentioned, usually, they are focused on the relationship that the women had or continue to maintain with their families. These intergenerational women are compassionate toward others, have strong religious views, and they have been known to have a zeal for tradition. The culture of Traditionalists and Baby Boomers focused on the value of education and imparting this idea to younger generations.

BIGGEST
INSPIRATION

"The future belongs to those who believe in the beauty of their dreams."
–Eleanor Roosevelt

# BIGGEST INSPIRATION

- Being a Christian. Although my immediate family is small, I have a huge Christian family which gives me much joy.

- My greatest inspiration in life was to achieve two goals: one, to be the first one out of eighteen siblings to complete high school. Second, was to become a cosmetologist. Through determination and hard work, I was able to achieve my first goal of obtaining my high school diploma. The second goal of becoming a cosmetologist took a little longer. By the time I was able to pursue my cosmetologist goal, I was married with three children. However, I was determined to make it happen so I enrolled in the beauty school and I was on my way to achieving my goal. Being married to a military man, I had to move, which caused me to quit school and move to another state. After relocating, I immediately enrolled in school and finally completed the requirements for obtaining a certificate of cosmetology.

- Stories in the Bible (Old and New Testament). No matter how hard it gets, it can get worse. If you have faith in God, He'll bring you through all your discomforts. This has been proven from days of old and today. You have to actively seek him through Jesus, then humbly ask for help.

- My first-grade teacher was my biggest inspiration. She was kind and a very sweet lady. She was interested in her students learning.

- All four of my children are members of the Lord's Church. There is nothing more important than a person's soul.

- My biggest inspiration was my husband. We met in our teens, married and later had children. He was the most positive and easygoing person. He had very little money, but he had a heart and personality of gold. He encouraged me to pursue my goals. He helped with anything that needed to be done in the home. He was a wonderful father to our children. During his illness and eventual death, he remained hopeful and in good spirits.

• My parents are definitely my biggest inspiration. My father lost his first family so he was completely dedicated to us, his second family. He passed at the age of 54, leaving a younger widow, my mom, and the five of us. She worked for twenty-five years to feed and shelter us and made sure we were all educated. A true inspiration!

• My biggest inspiration is the history of my ancestors. I find their ability to endure indescribable hardships simply re-markable. The ability to maintain a faith in God, love for another in the midst of enduring brutality is awesome and inspiring to me.

• My biggest inspiration is not giving up on yourself. I en-joy seeing young people continue their education after high school. It is an inspiration to see younger people be moti-vated to complete college regardless of the obstacles in their lives.

• My biggest inspiration is my spiritual relationship with God and Christian family and friends.

• My mother is my biggest inspiration. She took me to sum-mer reading at the library every summer. The Springdale Library had a program where you read a selection from ev-ery section of the Dewey Decimal System. I remember loving the variety. It allowed a poor small-town girl to experience the world. I was insatiable.

- My biggest inspiration is being able to work with children. They make one feel good when you can make them smile and gain their interest. They can say the smartest things and you wonder where it came from, but it gives you the biggest laugh.

- My mother taught me family values. She taught me to work hard, to get an education, and to love other people.

- My biggest inspiration were my parents. They showed me loving and Godly examples of fairness and love. My mom showed me by example how to be a strong and kind woman. Also, to be an independent thinker with strong decent values. My dad showed me by example: true love for family and friends.

- My biggest inspiration is the church, teaching and feeding my spirit. Fellowship with others for mutual support and camaraderie.

- My mother was widowed with three children after eight years of marriage. She had not completed high school. She was employed as a maid. She went back to high school and graduated. An employee saw promise and helped to get financial assistance to go to college (while still working as a maid). She finished undergraduate and graduate school.

- My mother became Dean of Women and a teacher at a newly established junior college in Texas. Although she never made much money (she still worked during the summers as a maid), the influence she had on many students and their families was outstanding. She always stressed education. I will always be amazed by her determination and hard work.

- My biggest inspiration was my parents and grandparents. Growing up watching and learning from them, including how they handled adversity, their love for life and people, their actions for social justice. Later in life, I read *Anyway: The Ten Paradoxical Commandments* by Dr. Kent M. Keith. It described what my parents and grandparents accomplished with their lives. It helped me understand how to move past the negative actions of others and maintain the energy to do the right thing, anyway. It continues to inspire me to be the kindest and most effective person possible.

- My biggest inspiration is loving life.

- My biggest inspiration was my parents and the elders in the small community. I grew up in North Carolina. It was a community of folk who practiced and preached faith, honesty, and service. My parents and the elders provided opportunities to share our time, possessions, energy, and gifts. They taught us that God loves a cheerful giver. I believed them then and I do now.

- My biggest inspiration was special unexpected meetings with complete strangers who have left me with a great feeling. It always inspired me to do my best and to show love. In those special moments of interaction with others, I feel God's presence.

- My biggest inspiration is any women who gracefully combine strength and excellence with compassion, understanding, and kindness.

- My mother was my biggest inspiration. Her expectations

and dreams for me were always in focus. My desire was not to disappoint her.

- My biggest inspiration is to succeed and not fail. I always tried to do my best, to be fair, and honest with all people. If I failed, I always wanted to feel I gave the best I had to give. Others might be able to do it better, but this was my best.
- My mother inspires me more than anyone or anything. Through the years, I've watched her cope with good, bad, happy, and sad. Yet, she always placed her trust in God no matter what. I've always known her to be truthful in every aspect, but being careful and tactful in how she presented the truth. Hopefully, I will in some way measure up to that.
- My parents taught me to strive to be independent and not depend on others for my success.
- My biggest inspiration is family (physical and spiritual). In my physical family, I am surrounded by three encouraging brothers and three other sisters who have served as cheerleaders for me in all my endeavors. In my spiritual family, of which I have been a part for fifty-two years, I am constantly given heartening words and phrases to keep my spirits up.
- God's unconditional love and grace is my greatest inspiration. It has inspired me to love and care for others as God has loved and cared for me. He has blessed me with my family, good health, and grace.
- My biggest inspiration was my third supervisor. She was always willing to help anyone, serve on any committee, take time to explain, and forgive others' failures. She stood up for herself and paved the way for other women in her field.

She showed that nice women finish first and have a great time doing it.

- My biggest inspiration was to become an actress. I was inspired by my peers. As a result, I pursued a minor in drama. I have starred in many local and area productions. It was my desire to make people laugh. Several of my roles led to making people laugh.

- My biggest inspiration is my relationship with Christ.

- My two children were my biggest inspiration. They always made me want to be a respectable person of good character, caring and giving. Very early, I taught them that character is how you treat those who can do nothing for you. Being there for my children kept me in touch with God and my spirituality. I wanted them to know love and have faith in the man that will never leave you. They are successful adults and their volunteer spirit inspires me.

- My biggest inspiration were my parents. They were hard workers, and they tried to get their children what they could not get or have when they were growing up. They tried to instill in us to be nice to people and not to think we were better than anyone else.

- I do not stress over what I aspired to be. When you trust God, you realize your most perfect plan is nothing compared to the providence of God. He knows what is best for you and the path you should take.

- Old generations inspire me. As a young child, I gravitated to older people. Presently, I am fortunate and blessed to remember some of the things that sounded so "farfetched."

- They were pearls of wisdom in disguise. I am blessed to

keep in touch with some of my mother's friends. Also, it is a privilege to speak or share a smile with older generations at the store. Calling and sending cards to older generations is a blessing.

- My father was my biggest inspiration. He instilled in my siblings and me the love of family. To love God above all others. Let God be the center of all you do. My father showed me the meaning of true love, trust, and faith.

- My mother was my biggest inspiration. When I was growing up, there were times when my father was out of work. My mother always "made do." She never made my sisters or I feel insecure. Frequently, she told us, God will take care of us.

- My biggest inspiration are my grandchildren. I enjoy watching my grandchildren going through life situations. I observe them not only making decisions and mistakes but growing from them. Also, I am grateful that I contributed to their lives.

# CONCLUSION

*"It takes a lot of courage to show your dreams to someone else."*

-Erma Bombeck

# CONCLUSION

Martha Graham, one of many women who helped shape the century, was asked how long she intended to continue dancing; she replied, "As long as I've got an audience." That's the spirit that should be noted when sharing life-learned lessons with younger women. Also, Martha Graham said that practice means to perform over and over again in the face of all obstacles, some act of vision, of faith, of desire. Practice is a means of inviting the perfection desired (Brainy Quotes, 2018).

According to Collins English Dictionary (n.d.), lifelong learning is the provision or use of both formal and informal learning opportunities throughout people's lives in order to foster the continuous development and improvement of the knowledge and skills needed for employment and personal fulfilment. The idea and concept of lifelong learning has been extended from generation to generation. Hopefully, Traditionalist and Baby Boomer generations of women will continue to advise and influence younger women. These intergenerational women have shared a wealth of life experiences. Most women continue to value relationships by balancing life along with community service and helping others (Harvard Business School, 2015).

The Life Experience Surveys were conducted from November 2017 through March 2018. Surveys were conducted regarding information about life experiences of Traditionalists and Baby Boomers. The purpose was to share these responses with women 18-35 years; however, women of all ages could benefit from this compiled data. These Traditionalist and Baby Boomer women were from a stratified random sample. Based on self-identified birthplace from respondents, twelve states were represented in the survey. This data was collected by self-report measures. Because the survey tool required self-disclosure, participants were assured of anonymity and data confidentiality. Participants were mailed a survey and they were requested to return the completed survey in a self-addressed envelope. Less than a third of participants requested a telephone interview. Only two participants requested a telephone interview.

Forty surveys were distributed to Traditionalist and Baby Boomer women.

The survey sampled approximately fourteen Traditionalist and twenty-three Baby Boomer women. The survey had a 92.5% response rate, which was considered to be high for a survey of its kind.

<h1 align="center">PARTICIPANT SURVEY</h1>

Name:
Place of birth:

Question 1: The best advice you ever received.
Answer:

Question 2: One word to describe your character.
Answer:

Question 3: What do you consider one of your most prized
possessions?
Answer:

Question 4: Your biggest inspiration (Explain the reason
for your response)
Answer:

This information will be used in a book to encourage
young women in life experiences.

Adapted by Lottie Adams from *Arkansas Democrat-Gazette*
(2017) Self Portrait

# REFERENCES

Anton Chekhov Quotes. (n.d.). BrainyQuote.com. Retrieved July 9, 2019, from BrainyQuote.com Web site: https://www. brainyquote.com/quotes/anton_chekhov_119060

Barr, C. How to Create a Vision for Your Life. Retrieved 11/1/17 from http://Corbettbar.com/how-to-create-a-vision-for-your -life/

Benjamin Franklin Quotes. (n.d.). BrainyQuote.com. Retrieved July 5, 2019, from

BrainyQuote.com Web site: https://www.brainyquote.com/quotes/ benjamin_franklin_103731

Covey, S.R. (1989). *The 7 habits of highly effective people.* Restoring the character ethic. Simon & Schuster. P.46

Eleanor Roosevelt Quotes. (n.d.). BrainyQuote.com. Retrieved July 5, 2019, from

BrainyQuote.com Web site:

https://www.brainyquote.com/quotes/eleanor_roosevelt_100940

Erma Bombeck Quotes. (n.d.). BrainyQuote.com. Rerieved July 9, 2019, from BrainyQuote.com Web site: https://www. brainyquote.com/quotes/erma_bombeck_130034

Faulkner, W. (n.d.). TOP 25 QUOTES BY WILLIAM FAULKNER (of 383): A-Z Quotes.

Retrieved from

https://www.azquotes.com/author/17609-William_Faulkner

Gelman, L. (2015). Art of living: The best advice I ever got. *Reader's Digest*. Vol.185. Issue 1107 (pp.41-47). Harlan, IA

Georgia O'Keeffe Quotes. (n.d.). BrainyQuote.com. Retrieved July 5, 2019, from BrainyQuote.com Web site: https://www.brainyquote.com/quotes/georgia_okeeffe_119602

Lifelong learning. (n.d.). Collins English Dictionary - Complete & Unabridged 10th edition. Retrieved January 22, 2018 from Dictionary.com website: http://www.dictionary.com/browse/lifelong-learning

Mark Twain Quotes. (n.d.). BrainyQuote.com. Retrieved July 5, 2019, from BrainyQuote.com Web site: https://www.brainyquote.com/quotes/mark_twain_118964

Martha Graham Quotes. (n.d.). BrainyQuote.com. Retrieved July 9, 2019, from BrainyQuote.com Web site: https://www.brainyquote.com/quotes/ martha_graham_113628

Maya Angelou Quotes. (n.d.). BrainyQuote.com. Retrieved July 5, 2019, from BrainyQuote.com Web site: https://www.brainyquote.com/quotes/maya_angelou_578808

Ralph Waldo Emerson Quotes. (n.d.). BrainyQuote.com. Retrieved July 5, 2019, from BrainyQuote.com Web site: https://www.brainyquote.com/quotes/ralph_waldo_emerson_122708

Random House Webster's Unabridged Dictionary. (2001). Second Edition. Random House. New York.

Tea, M. (2015). *How to grow up*. New York: Penguin Group (USA) LLC

ValueOptions.com/spotlight_ retrieved on 12/6/2017YIW/traditional.htm

About the Author

Lottie L. Adams, Ed.D. resides in Jacksonville, Arkansas and is a retired registered nurse and administrator for the Arkansas Department of Health. After thirty-five years, she retired from this profession. Later, she worked as an adjunct college professor for Embry-Riddle, Strayer University, and Webster University. During the span of her lifelong education, she earned an Associate of Science Degree in Nursing from University of Arkansas at Little Rock, Bachelor of Science in Social Psychology from Park University, A Master's Degree in Public Administration and Human Resource Development from Webster University, and a Doctorate of Education in Organizational Leadership with a specialty in Conflict Resolution and Mediation and Negotiation from Nova Southeastern University. Professional Organizations: American Association of University Women and Southwestern Christian College.